THIS WALKER BOOK BELONGS TO:

_____

_____

_____

WELL 'ARD!

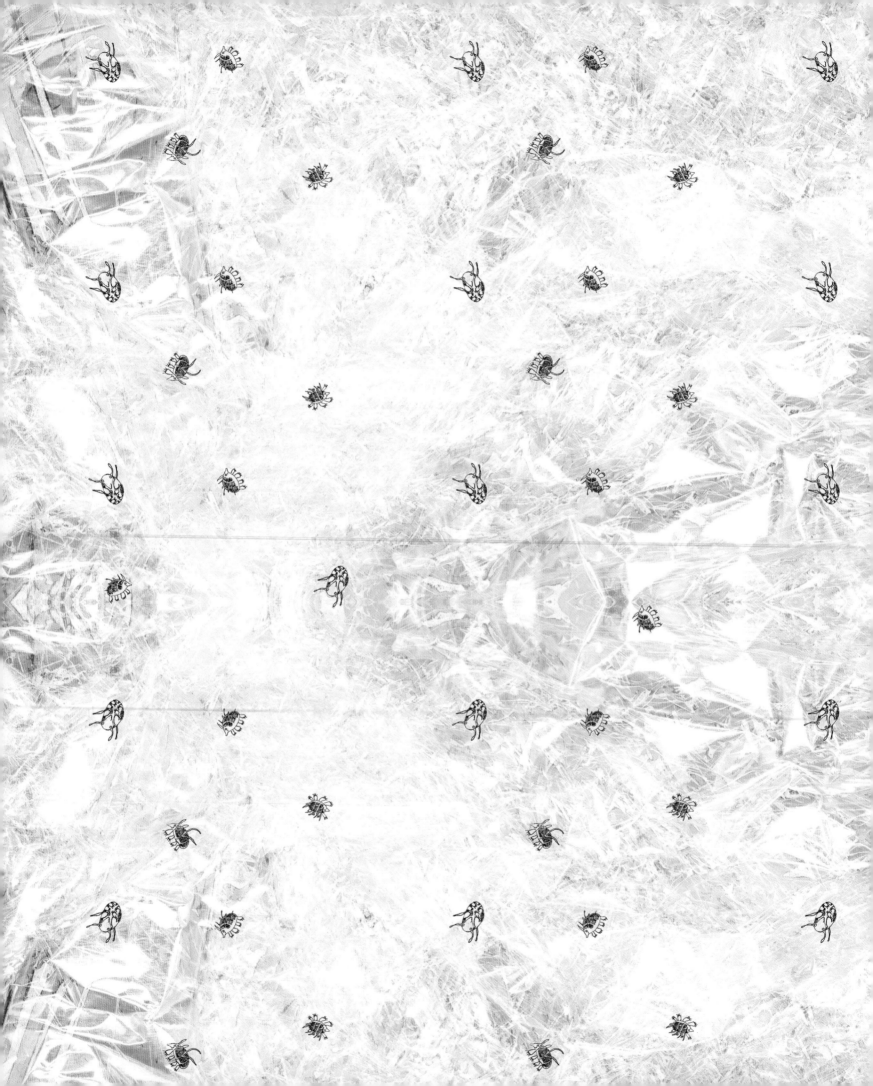

For
Mike Shooter, with love N.D.

For
Alison – I'd be frozen, boiled and squashed without you N.L.

THE TINY BACTERIA ON THE OPPOSITE PAGE ARE ENJOYING BEING BOOBED ALIVE IN SUPER HOT MUD. YOU CAN FIND OUT WHY IF YOU TURN TO PAGE 21...

First published 2006 by Walker Books Ltd, 87 Vauxhall Walk, London SE11 5HJ

This edition published 2014

10 9 8 7 6 5 4 3 2 1

Text © 2006 Nicola Davies   Illustrations © 2006 Neal Layton

The right of Nicola Davies and Neal Layton to be identified as author and illustrator respectively of this work has been asserted by them in accordance with the Copyright, Designs and Patents Act 1988

This book has been typeset in AT Arta

Printed in China

British Library Cataloguing in Publication Data: a catalogue record for this book is available from the British Library

ISBN 978-1-4063-5665-6

www.walker.co.uk

Survivors

The Toughest Creatures on Earth

by **Nicola Davies**

illustrated by **Neal Layton**

WALKER BOOKS

AND SUBSIDIARIES

LONDON • BOSTON • SYDNEY • AUCKLAND

WHAT A BUNCH OF WIMPS

We humans are such a bunch of sissies!

We can't stand the cold ...

we can't stand the heat ...

we can't do without food, or water ...

and a few minutes without air is enough to finish us off.

Luckily, not all life is so fragile. All over the planet there are animals (and plants) that relish the sort of conditions that would kill a human, quicker than you could say "coffin".

KEEPING OUT THE FREEZE

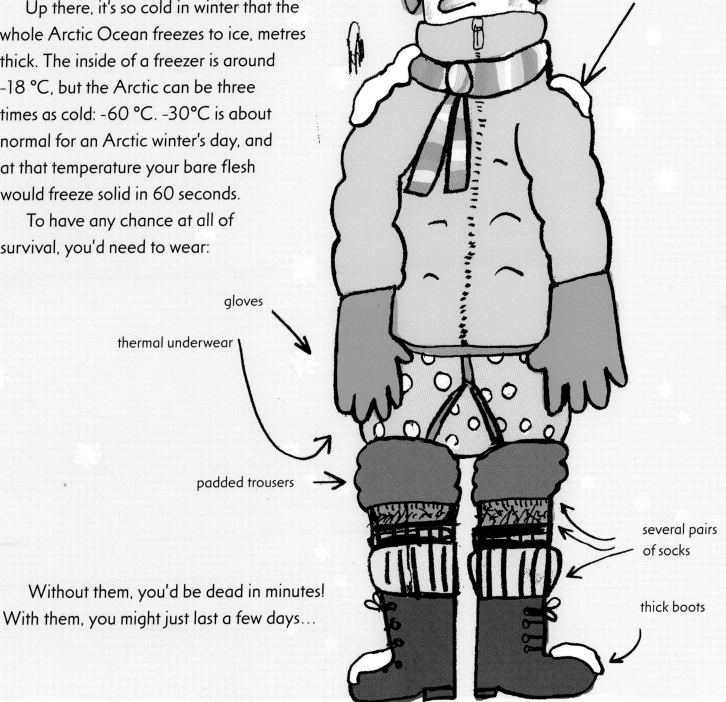

a hat

an extra hat

a down jacket and a fleece

gloves

thermal underwear

padded trousers

several pairs of socks

thick boots

Let's start at the top, the top of our world: the Arctic region – where the North Pole is.

Up there, it's so cold in winter that the whole Arctic Ocean freezes to ice, metres thick. The inside of a freezer is around -18 °C, but the Arctic can be three times as cold: -60 °C. -30°C is about normal for an Arctic winter's day, and at that temperature your bare flesh would freeze solid in 60 seconds.

To have any chance at all of survival, you'd need to wear:

Without them, you'd be dead in minutes! With them, you might just last a few days…

Yet polar bears stay constantly cosy ... in the nude! That's because their birthday suits work better than our clothes. Instead of thermal underwear, polar bears have a 7 cm layer of fat under their skin. Over that, they have a double layer of fur, which has an extra trick for beating cold: each hair is hollow, not white at all, and traps warm air like a mini duvet. Polar bear skin too is special: it's black! Dark colours absorb more heat than light colours – just take a walk in a black T-shirt on a hot day if you don't believe me – so any warmth that the fur traps, soaks back into the bear's body.

This all works so well that it fooled some scientists, who decided that the best way to count bears was to scan the snow, from a plane, with heat-sensitive cameras. The snag was that polar bear body heat is so locked in that the outside of the fur is the same temperature as the snow. So the only thing that showed up was the occasional polar bear nose – they're not covered in fur!

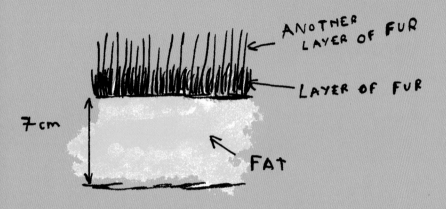

ANOTHER LAYER OF FUR

LAYER OF FUR

7 cm

FAT

POLAR BEAR FAT/FUR DIAGRAM

GRRR!!

I THINK I CAN SEE SOMETHING...

WORLD'S COSIEST COAT

Polar bear fur could be the warmest on Earth, but there are other contenders for the title of World's Cosiest Coat.

Arctic musk oxen have the warmest woolly coats. Their wool grows right down to their ankles and it's eight times warmer than sheep's wool. (It even has a special name: qiviut, that's KEE-vee-ut.)

Sea otters have the densest fur on Earth, with about 155,000 hairs per square centimetre. They spend all their lives in extremely cold water and their fine fur keeps a layer of warm air trapped next to their skin all the time.

Bowhead whales live in the Arctic Ocean, where the water is almost freezing all year round.

Of course they don't have any fur at all, but they do have a layer of fat under the skin half a metre thick. You could say that's the thickest underwear in the world.

But the title would probably have to go to the emperor penguin's coat of feathers. Emperor penguins live at the other end of the planet, the South Pole. The Antarctic is the coldest place on Earth, where winter temperatures are between -20 and -88°C. And winter is when emperor penguins choose to breed!

9

EMPEROR PENGUIN DIAGRAM

There's nowhere to nest, and nothing to make a nest with, so male emperor penguins just balance the one egg, which their mate has laid, on their feet. Then they stand around in the snow and hundred-mile-an-hour freezing winds for 65 days, until it hatches.

This sounds impossible – not to mention miserable and boring – but emperor dads manage it because of their amazing coat of feathers. It's 3 cm thick, with stiff feathers to keep the wind out and fluffy feathers to keep the warmth in. The coat is so good at keeping heat in and cold out, that there can be a temperature difference of 60 °C between the inside and outside of the feathers.

A feathery fold of skin keeps the egg cosy. But daddy penguins' feet have no heat-saving cover. So, to stop their body heat leaking out that way, they use a "counter-current mechanism". This is a swanky name for the way that warm blood going to the feet gives most of its heat to the cold blood coming from the feet, and going back into the body. So the feet are kept just warmer than freezing, but very little precious body heat ends up escaping through the tootsies.

10

COLD CUDDLING

Having a warm coat isn't the only way to cheat life-threatening cold. Sharing your body heat works brilliantly. Emperor penguins do it, gathering together in their hundreds to beat the Antarctic chill. Very, very slowly, the penguins shuffle along, changing position, so that everyone gets a turn in the warm centre of the huddle.

For very small birds, even an ordinary, frosty winter night can be life-threateningly cold. Tiny birds like wrens just can't keep warm, so up to thirty of them will roost together. Cuddled up, they can survive temperatures that would have frozen them to the branch by morning.

Many birds and other animals use huddling to keep warm, but Inca doves from the south-western United States and Mexico are the only ones that do it in formation: they make themselves into a living pyramid to warm up after the deep chill of winter nights.

TRUE TOUGHNESS

Polar bears can keep warm in conditions that would kill a human, but even they would die if their body temperature dropped by more than a few degrees. The truth is that, inside its big coat, a polar bear is just as much of a sissy as we are. The Truly Tough Animals are the ones that can let their bodies get cold right through, and still survive.

Some of the most delicate creatures on Earth are in fact Truly Tough. Hummingbirds let their body temperatures drop 20 or 30 degrees below normal. Just compare that with humans: if our temperature drops by 2 °C we get ill, and a drop of 10 °C is likely to kill us. Yet hummingbirds do it almost every night to save on food. Keeping their bodies warm would burn food, and hummingbirds can't fly around feeding on nectar in the dark!

Food-saving makes some bats Truly Tough too. Insects disappear in winter, so the bats that eat them must live off their own body fat. Keeping warm and active would burn those fat stores too fast, so bats hibernate and let their bodies get really cold, to make their fat stores last until spring. Red bats from Canada and the US get the coldest and can stand a body temperature down to -5 °C for a short time. But that's their limit — any colder and they start to burn fat to warm up again.

12

FROG LOLLIES

Mammals and birds are warm-blooded, so they can burn food to keep warm. But other animals – such as reptiles and amphibians – are cold-blooded, and can't keep warm that way. The only way they can survive freezing temperatures is by hiding somewhere warm, or by turning into an icicle for the winter!

Down in the freezing leaf litter of the forests where the red bats hibernate, you can find wood frogs, frozen solid and brittle as glass. These "frogsicles" aren't dead, and in the springtime they will just thaw out and hop off into the sunshine.

Usually, being frozen solid is very, very bad for living things. That's because bodies are mostly made of water. When water freezes to ice – at a little below 0 °C – it expands (gets bigger) and breaks whatever happens to be holding it. (This is why water pipes in houses sometimes burst in frosty weather.) When bodies freeze, ice bursts blood vessels and wrecks organs, like hearts and lungs, by cracking open their cells. (Cells are the tiny, delicate building blocks from which all bodies are made.)

How, then, do "frogsicles" survive? They do it by making the ice grow *between* all the important bits of their bodies, *outside* those teeny cells, where it can't do much harm.

ANTIFREEZE

(OR, PUT SOME BEETLE BLOOD IN YOUR CAR)

If an animal can't keep warm, or survive turning to ice, what does it do in extreme cold? It uses antifreeze. Some animal antifreezes work in just the same way as the antifreeze we put in our cars: they make water freeze at a much lower temperature, so even if it gets colder than freezing, there's no ice formation.

Wood frogs use sugar as antifreeze! They fill the water in their cells with it, lowering the freezing point way below zero, so that ice can't form and damage their bodies. But some fish have antifreeze that works in an even cleverer way: by sticking to ice crystals, so they can't grow! Ice fish from the Antarctic Ocean live in water that is colder than the freezing point of most fish blood. But ice fish, and other fish like them, don't freeze, because their bodies are full of this clever antifreeze.

Polar seas don't ever get colder than a few degrees below freezing, but on land, Arctic and Antarctic temperatures can go down to -30 °C, -60 °C or even -80 °C. Resisting freezing in those conditions needs a very strong antifreeze indeed. And that is just what scientists have found in some polar insects. Some Arctic beetles and tiny Antarctic springtails, just a few millimetres long, stay unfrozen in extreme polar cold because their ice-eating antifreeze is thirty times stronger than the one in fish! (Scientists get very excited about animal antifreezes because they hope to be able to copy them, to help us humans preserve food, and to keep organs for transplant alive for much longer.)

BLOWING HOT AND COLD

Snowy poles and mountain-tops aren't the only places where it gets horribly cold. Deserts can freeze at night because there's no cloud to keep the warmth in once the sun goes down. This gives desert animals a bit of a problem: it may be too hot by day for a thick coat of fur or feathers, so what do you do about the night-time chill?

Roadrunners, long-legged birds from the deserts of the southern United States, put up with the night-time cold only because they can get warm as soon as the sun rises. They turn their backs on the morning sun and lift their feathers so the nice warm rays shine onto a special strip of black skin across their shoulders. This soaks up the heat and warms each bird through, like a heated shawl! In no time at all, they're warm as toast and running about the desert at top speed.

THE CAMEL YO-YO

Camels use the desert climate in the opposite way to roadrunners. The coldness of the night actually helps them to survive the high temperatures of the day, which can be 45 or 50 °C. We humans get ill if our temperatures go up more than a couple of degrees, and a rise of 6 °C can be lethal. But camels let theirs go up and down like yo-yos, by as much as 8 °C. At sunrise, after a chilly night, camels' bodies are quite cool. They get warmer and warmer all day, but by the time they're getting a bit too hot, the sun goes down and night cools them off again.

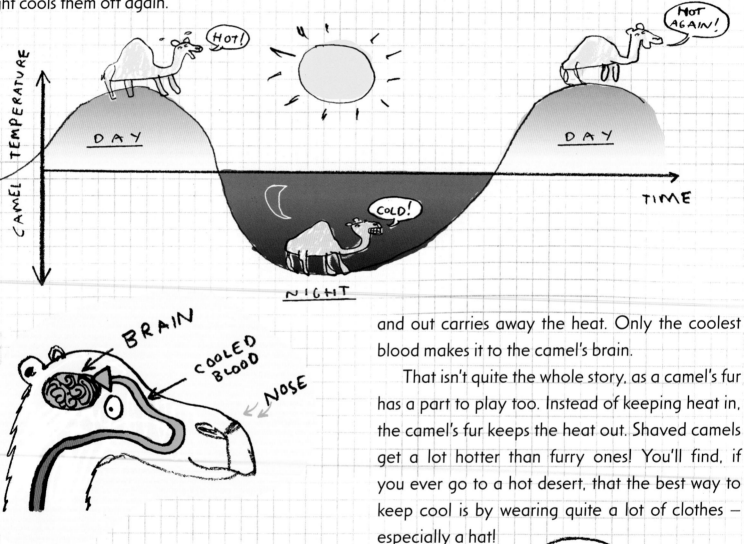

The one part of a camel that can't cope with the daytime temperature rise of 8 °C is the brain. If it gets as hot as the rest of the camel, the brain will start to die. So blood on its way to the camel's brain is cooled by passing through blood vessels in the camel's long nose, where the air moving in and out carries away the heat. Only the coolest blood makes it to the camel's brain.

That isn't quite the whole story, as a camel's fur has a part to play too. Instead of keeping heat in, the camel's fur keeps the heat out. Shaved camels get a lot hotter than furry ones! You'll find, if you ever go to a hot desert, that the best way to keep cool is by wearing quite a lot of clothes – especially a hat!

HOW TO LIVE IN A DESERT

Letting your body temperature go up and down is a good way to cope with desert life. But most mammals can't do it. Our bodies just don't work properly unless we stay at a pretty even temperature. So desert mammals — apart from camels of course — tend to stay hidden underground, where it's cooler, by day. They come out at night, when their ability to burn food and keep their bodies warm is useful.

Reptiles don't mind yo-yoing body temperatures, they're used to it. They can't make their own body heat, so they rely on the sun to warm them up and the shade to cool them down. They can't move around quickly when their bodies are chilled, so mostly they spend nights underground (out of the way of hungry mammals). They come out when there's sunshine to warm them. Many are quite comfortable if their body temperature goes up to over 38 °C. Desert iguanas from the US are happy up to 46 °C, but if they start getting hotter than that, they have to lie down in the shade!

In the Sahara Desert in Africa, just as the reptiles run for cover, the ants come out. Silver ants can cope with a body temperature of 53 °C, a few degrees more than the fringe-fingered lizards that like to eat them. So the ants can search for food without being eaten, and claim the title of Hottest Animal in the Desert.

DYING FOR A DRINK

Heat isn't the biggest problem in deserts. Lack of water is. In 45 °C desert heat you would need to sweat as much as 3.5 litres EVERY HOUR to stop your body overheating. Camels, when they have plenty of water to drink, don't bother with all that body heat yo-yo stuff, they just sweat and sweat to keep cool.

But remember the main feature of deserts? Right! NO water (which is why camels in the desert don't just sweat to keep cool. A camel's hump, by the way, is fat: a store of food, not water). And without water to replace all you'd lose in sweat, you'd dry out like a prune, then overheat too and be dead in about a day.

Camels are comfortable with losing a quarter of their bodies' water, but humans and most other mammals can't tolerate losing much more than a tenth. What with that and not being able to put up with body temperatures of more than a few degrees above normal (unless they're a camel, of course), mammals are doubly bad at desert living. But reptiles, as we've seen already, don't mind getting hot and so don't need to sweat to keep cool. They're also very resistant to drying out. For a start, they have thick, scaly skins that keep water safely inside their bodies. On top of that, they have special wee that uses up very little water. And, as a final aid to surviving heat and drought, desert reptiles can put up with losing most of their bodies' water, so they can survive for many months without drinking at all!

A REPTILE DIAGRAM

FRIED, DRIED AND STARVED!

Reptiles are suited to desert life in another way too: they're good at going without food! Mammals use energy to keep their bodies from getting too cold or too hot, so they need ten times more food than reptiles to keep them alive. And as food can be in short supply in a desert, being able to put up with starvation is very useful.

Insects and spiders are cold-blooded too, and even better at starving than reptiles, as a British naturalist, John Blackwell, found out over 170 years ago. He put a spider in a jar on 15 October 1829, and it lived without food or water until 30 April 1831, more than 18 months later! That's just the sort of survival skill you need for hanging around in webs in the corner of a room, hoping that a fly might pass!

Humans, like most mammals and birds, are rubbish at starving. The longest an average-sized adult human could expect to last without food would be around 40 days. But not all warm-blooded animals are so bad at it. Emperor penguins don't eat at all while they are incubating, nor on the long journey back to the sea after their eggs hatch. That's a total of 115 days without food! Polar bears can endure up to 8 months without food. They use up all their fat reserves and even some of their muscles, so they are almost eating themselves alive.

Burning up your own body as food allows animals to survive times when food is scarce, but it's useful in other ways too: it can help with long-distance travel! Tiny blackpoll warblers migrate from North America to South America, in an 80-hour, non-stop flight. It's the equivalent of a human running 1,200 four-minute miles! The warblers do it by using their own bodies as fuel, so by the time they arrive, they are not much more than bone and feather, and have lost half their body weight!

INTO THE INFERNO

Polar wastes, desiccated deserts and the insides of old glass jars! Is there anywhere on Earth that animals can't live? What about volcanoes? Molten magma, boiling pools of mud and spouts of scalding water, all clouded in deadly gases — you'd think *nothing* could survive in such places. Well, you'd be wrong. If you could get close enough to look, without being burnt to death, you'd see smears of colour in the mud and water: red, orange, cloudy grey and blue. These are colonies of bacteria, tiny living beings whose whole bodies are just one cell.

Bacteria live everywhere, but the bacteria that live near volcanoes are special. They are called "thermophiles" (which means "heat-lovers") and they can *only* live where it's hot enough to boil water — between 80 °C and 110 °C. Thermophiles don't only love being boiled, many enjoy being suffocated and poisoned too! Most eat chemicals like sulphur and iron for energy, and nearly all would be killed by contact with ordinary oxygen. How do these tiny single-celled beings survive? Nobody knows exactly *how*, but scientists do know *why*: billions of years ago, when thermophiles evolved, Earth was covered in volcanoes and boiling seas of sulphuric acid, there wasn't even any air, just poisonous gas. As far as thermophiles are concerned, things haven't changed a bit!

CLOSE-UP OF THERMOPHILE BACTERIA

IRON
SULPHUR
YUM!

21

BLACK SMOKERS

Thermophiles live wherever the hot, melted heart of the Earth bubbles up, even at the very bottom of the sea. Down there, you can find plumes of super-hot water streaming up from the molten rock below. These are called "black smokers", and thermophiles live here in their millions, bathing in the boiling water and eating chemicals. They aren't alone either. Where cold sea-water cools the super-heated plumes, eyeless shrimps, giant worms and other weird creatures eat the thermophiles, and each other! It's a whole other world that doesn't need sunlight, and would go on existing even if our sun went out. Black smokers could even give us some clues about how life might exist on other planets.

THE SQUASH FACTOR

In fact, scientists actually know more about the surface of the moon than they know about the very bottom of our own oceans. One reason for that is pressure – the squash factor. The deeper you go under the ocean, the greater the weight of water pressing down on you. For every 10 metres you go down, the pressure increases by what's called one "atmosphere". So if you were to dive to the deepest place in the ocean, the bottom of the Mariana Trench, 11 km below the surface, there would be 1,100 atmospheres pressing down on you. All the air-filled bits of your body, like your lungs and ribcage, would be squashed flat, and you'd be unable to breathe. You'd also suffer from High Pressure Nervous Syndrome (HPNS) which would make you shake uncontrollably and pass out a lot.

Instead, you would need to go down in something that looks more like a spacecraft from a science-fiction movie: a submersible, with a very thick hull to resist that super-squashing pressure and big headlights to see with, because the deep sea is completely dark. All sorts of weird and wonderful animals would loom in the headlights: hatchet fish, gulper eels and tripod fish, luminous squid and starfish on stalks. And not one of them would seem bothered by that huge weight of water. They certainly wouldn't look squashed. That's because they don't have air-filled bits of body, like lungs, to squash! What's more, their nervous systems are adapted for life at depth; they get the symptoms of HPNS in shallow water!

BUBBLES IN THE BLOOD

You probably don't need to be reminded that humans have to breathe air, so if we want to stay under water for longer than a couple of minutes, we have to take our air supply with us. And that air supply has to be under the same pressure as the pressure of water squashing our ribcages – or it wouldn't stand a chance of getting into our lungs. Under high pressure like that, air can dissolve in the blood. As soon as a deep-sea diver comes back to the surface and the pressure is off, that air re-forms as bubbles. Think of a pop bottle with the lid firmly on and the drink inside under pressure: take off the lid and there's an immediate fizz of bubbles. Now imagine that happening to the human body. Ouch! It's very painful and potentially fatal. It's called "the bends" and human divers have to come to the surface very slowly to avoid it.

Yet sperm whales dive to depths of more than 1,000 metres and elephant seals go down to 1,570 metres, and all without a touch of the bends! How? Both whales and seals breathe out when they dive, then, at around 50 metres below the surface, their ribs fold flat and their lungs are squashed empty. So there's no air in the lungs to be forced into their blood. This way they can stay down for 30 to 50 minutes and pop back up without the ghost of a fizz. (And how do they manage without breathing for so long? By storing oxygen in their blood and muscles before they dive!)

25

FEEL THE FORCE OF "G"

SPLAT!!

If you do decide that exploring space seems less risky than exploring the deep ocean, you will have to deal with another kind of squash factor. You've probably experienced it already if you've been on a fast fairground ride – the ride spins faster and faster and you are pressed into your seat, as if someone were sitting on your chest! This is the effect of the "g-force". Gravity is the force that stops you falling off the Earth and makes buttered toast drop on the floor (though the reason it falls buttered-side down is due to something different – Murphy's Law). Gravity is measured in "g"s. Just standing still, a force of 1 g is what keeps your feet on the ground. If you start to accelerate, in a fairground ride for instance, or even worse a jet aircraft, the g-force grows. It pins you into your seat and pulls all your blood to your feet. At around 5 g, the blood just can't make it to your brain any more and you pass out. Fighter pilots in World War II experienced huge g-forces when flying fast turns, and regularly blacked out.

Nowadays, jet plane pilots wear a special "g suit", which squeezes the blood up from their legs to their heads. All the same, US Air Force recruits must pass a test that shows they can stay conscious at 7.5 g for 16 seconds. The maximum g-force the human skeleton can stand is 25 g – any more than that and our bones start to break!

In the insect world, 25 g is nothing. A flea can jump 130 times its own height, somersaulting at high speed as it does, and experiencing a force of 200 g. Click beetles can jump even faster and survive 400 g. As the click beetle spins in the air, its head suffers up to 2,000 g, yet click beetles never seem to pass out! (The scientist who measured this says that click beetle brains aren't damaged, as ours would be, because click beetles aren't very bright anyway!)

SPONGE SMOOTHIE AND THE HISTORY OF LIFE

Whales and click beetles suffer huge squashing forces and still stay in one piece. They are really just squash resistors. To be a Truly Tough Animal, you have to be a squash survivor, and stay alive even if your body is in bits! Quite a lot of invertebrates (that's animals without bones, like insects, worms, crabs and snails) are good at this, because their bodies are simple and easier to make. Worms can be chopped in two and grow a new other half. Starfish can be cut to bits and each bit will become a new starfish (something that divers in Australia found out rather too late, when they tried to get rid of a plague of crown-of-thorns starfish on the Great Barrier Reef by chopping them up).

Sponges are the toughest of all. They live in the sea and come in all shapes and sizes, from tiny flat ones to huge chimney-shaped ones. You might even have used the dead, rubbery insides of one to wash yourself in the bath! To be honest, even live sponges don't do much: they just sort of sit there and grow. But put one in a blender and you'll see that they do something no other animal can: pour your sponge smoothie back into its sea-water home, and it will put itself back together. All the tiny little bits of sponge will find each other and slowly rebuild the whole animal!

The reason that sponges can do this is an important part of the history of life on Earth...

ONCE UPON A TIME ...

all living things were tiny, just one cell big, like bacteria. Then some of these single-celled beings started living together in colonies and found that things were easier if some cells got food, and the others did the cleaning (as it were). Over time, these colonies got bigger and more complicated, with more and more different jobs. At last, cells in these colonies couldn't survive on their own: they'd become a multicellular organism, a being made of lots of different cells.

(Sponges are from an early part of this story. We have thousands of different kinds of cells in our bodies, but sponges only have about four. Their cells aren't completely helpless on their own, as one of our body cells would be, but they do like living together. So, when they get parted in the blender, they find their way back to each other, just as the first colonies of cells did millions of years ago.)

And they all lived happily ever after.

Except they didn't, because not even the Princess and the Handsome Prince live EVER after. Living things can resist cold, heat and pressure, starvation, poisoning and suffocation, but they can't resist time. In the end, time gets us all.

A YEW TREE

GIANT ALDABRAN TORTOISE

A TEACHER

A BRISTLE CONE PINE TREE THAT LIVES IN NEVADA

HOLDING BACK TIME

Living bodies only need to last long enough to reproduce and see their offspring safely into the world. So animals like humans and elephants, that take ages bringing up their young, do well in the Time Resistance stakes. We can expect to live 70 years or more – great compared with mice, who raise their babies in weeks and are lucky to see their second birthdays. But the longest-lived creatures live twice as long as humans, perhaps more. The slow-maturing giant Aldabran tortoise can live to be at least 152 years old, and recent discoveries suggest that bowhead whales can live to be over

ARE WE THERE YET..?

ALPHA CENTAURI

PLANET EARTH

200. However the most ancient animal could be the much smaller freshwater pearl mussel, which might live for several hundred years.

Compared with the longest-lived plants, however, these creatures are only babies. Yew trees, the big, sombre trees you see in British churchyards, can live for more than 1,000 years. But the oldest trees live in Nevada and California in the US. They are bristle cone pines, and scientists think they could have been growing for 5,000 years – which would make them even older than most teachers!

TIME TRAVELLERS

Studying how living things survive in volcanoes, or in the sunless depths of the sea, gives us a glimpse of what life might be like on other planets; studying how plants and animals survive time might help us to travel to those planets.

Space is vast. Even light, the fastest thing in the universe, takes four years and three months to get here from our nearest star, Alpha Centauri (actually three stars together). Human spacecraft travel a lot more slowly than light. It took *Mars Express* nearly seven months to get to Mars, which is about two minutes away at light speed. So it would take a human spacecraft many, many years to travel to Alpha Centauri. If we want to go even further, it's going to take several human lifetimes of reading in-flight magazines.

We need to be able to do what some seeds can do – go into a state where life is kept on hold. Some seeds can lie dormant for hundreds, or even thousands, of years. A seed of the sacred lotus plant sprouted and grew after lying in a lake in China for more than 1,200 years. Seeds of sorghum, a tropical crop plant, can survive 6,000 years of waiting and still spring to life.

How do they do it? Scientists are still trying to find out, so it'll be quite a while before humans are "boldly going" anywhere far in the real Universe.

THE TOUGHEST CREATURE ON EARTH

In this book we've been all over the planet, to deserts, poles, mountain-tops, volcanoes, and even to the bottom of the sea, to find living things that are much, much tougher than human beings. But if you want to find the Truly Toughest Extreme Animal, the all-round champion, that can survive being frozen, boiled, squashed, and quite a few other trials besides, you probably don't need to go further than your local park or garden.

This celebrity creature lives quietly in films of water on plant leaves. (You could also find it in ponds, or in the sea.) It isn't big or spectacular, the largest is just over 1mm long. Its tiny, rounded body is divided into segments, and it has four pairs of little fat legs. It is a water bear, or tardigrade.

Tardigrades don't have big eyes or fluffy fur, but there is something rather cute about them. They are mysterious little creatures, belonging to a very ancient group of animals that appeared on Earth more than 530 million years ago!

During their long history on Earth, tardigrades have evolved to survive anything by entering a state scientists call "cryptobiosis" (which means "hidden life"). At the first sign of trouble – a spot of drought or a cold snap – tardigrades pull in their limbs and fold up their whole bodies, like a telescope. They fill their cells with sugar to preserve them, like the sugar in jam, and they dry out, losing all but one percent of their bodies' water. In this state, which is called a tun, they seem indestructible.

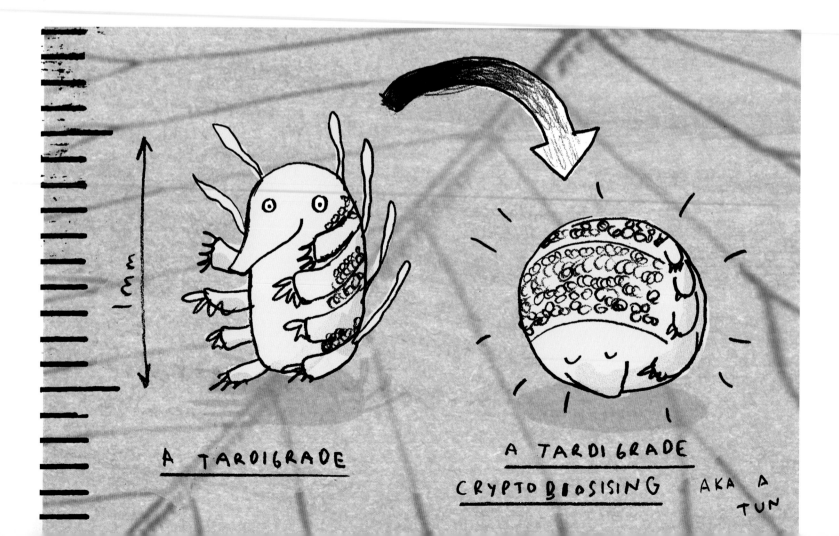

A TARDIGRADE

A TARDIGRADE
CRYPTOBIOSISING   AKA A
TUN

THE TOUGHEST ANIMAL ON EARTH

Scientists have heated tuns to 150 °C: that's one and a half times boiling point. They've frozen them to "absolute zero", the lowest possible temperature in the Universe, -272.8 °C. They've put them under six times the pressure you'd find at the bottom of the ocean, and under no pressure at all, like the vacuum of outer space. They've zapped them with X-rays a thousand times stronger than a lethal dose for humans, and they've poisoned them with chemicals. The result is always the same: when the danger is past and the tun is returned to its home in the water, its limbs pop out, its body unfolds and it goes about its business as if nothing at all had happened. There is even evidence to suggest that tuns could survive in their cryptobiotic state for hundreds, or even thousands, of years, making tardigrades almost immortal.

Tardigrade tuns are so tiny and light that they can blow around the planet in the wind. Perhaps they could travel high into the atmosphere and possibly even further! Could it be that the first Earthling to colonize another world in space will be a tardigrade?

They're certainly tough enough!

INDEX

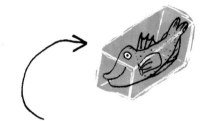

IT'S ME AGAIN!!

GLOSSARY

Antarctic the cold, frozen region around the South Pole, where penguins live.

Arctic the cold, frozen region around the North Pole, where polar bears live.

Bacteria tiny living things whose bodies are made from just one simple cell.

Black smokers cracks in the sea bed where super-hot mineral-rich water streams up like smoke.

Cells tiny units, too small to see, from which all living bodies are made.

Cold-blooded not being able to keep warm when it's cold or cool when it's hot. The body temperatures of reptiles, amphibians and fish go up and down with the temperature of their environment.

Dormancy a sleep-like state. Dormant seeds and plants are alive, but not growing, and can survive like that for years.

Hibernation how some animals survive the winter: they go into a deep sleep for weeks or even months, using up their body fat instead of eating.

Incubation keeping eggs warm so a baby can grow inside.

Magma red-hot melted rock that fills the centre of the Earth like the filling in a chocolate.

Organs groups of different sorts of cells working together to do a job. The brain, heart, lungs, liver, skin and kidneys are all organs.

Warm-blooded being able to keep warm when it's cold or cool when it's hot. Birds and mammals are warm-blooded.

ABOUT THE AUTHOR

Nicola Davies is an award-winning author, whose many books for children include *The Promise*, *A First Book of Nature*, *Big Blue Whale*, *Dolphin Baby* and *The Lion Who Stole My Arm*. She graduated in zoology, studied whales and bats, and then worked for the BBC Natural History Unit. Visit Nicola at **www.nicola-davies.com**

"The idea for *Survivors* came when I went to the Arctic," she says. "In spite of having lots of hi-tech, cold-beating clothing, I was freezing all the time. But the animals I saw had only their own bodies to keep out the cold and seemed perfectly happy. It got me wondering about the other very uncomfortable places that animals and plants thrive in."

ABOUT THE ILLUSTRATOR

Neal Layton is an award-winning artist who has illustrated more than sixty books for children, including the other titles in the Animal Science series. He also writes and illustrates his own books, such as *The Story of Everything* and The Mammoth Academy series. Visit Neal at **www.neallayton.co.uk**

"I enjoyed illustrating *Survivors* very much," he says. "Visualizing some of the science was a real challenge, and I learnt a lot too. I'd never heard of tardigrades before. Now they're one of my favourite animals."

SOURCES

This book is mostly pictures but gives a fascinating insight into what it's really like at the Poles:

Frozen Planet by Alastair Fothergill, Vanessa Berlowitz and David Attenborough (BBC Books, 2011)

Also:

Survival at 40°C Above by Debbie S. Miller and Jon Van Zyle (A&C Black Childrens & Educational, 2013)

Giant Tube Worms and Other Interesting Invertebrates by Heidi Moore (Raintree Publications, 2011)

This book is pretty grown up but you can dip in and out of it and you'll learn loads:

Animal Kingdom: Life in the Wild – How Wild Animals Survive in Their Different Habitats, from Deserts and Jungles to Oceans and the Skies by Michael Chinery (Lorenz Books, 2011)

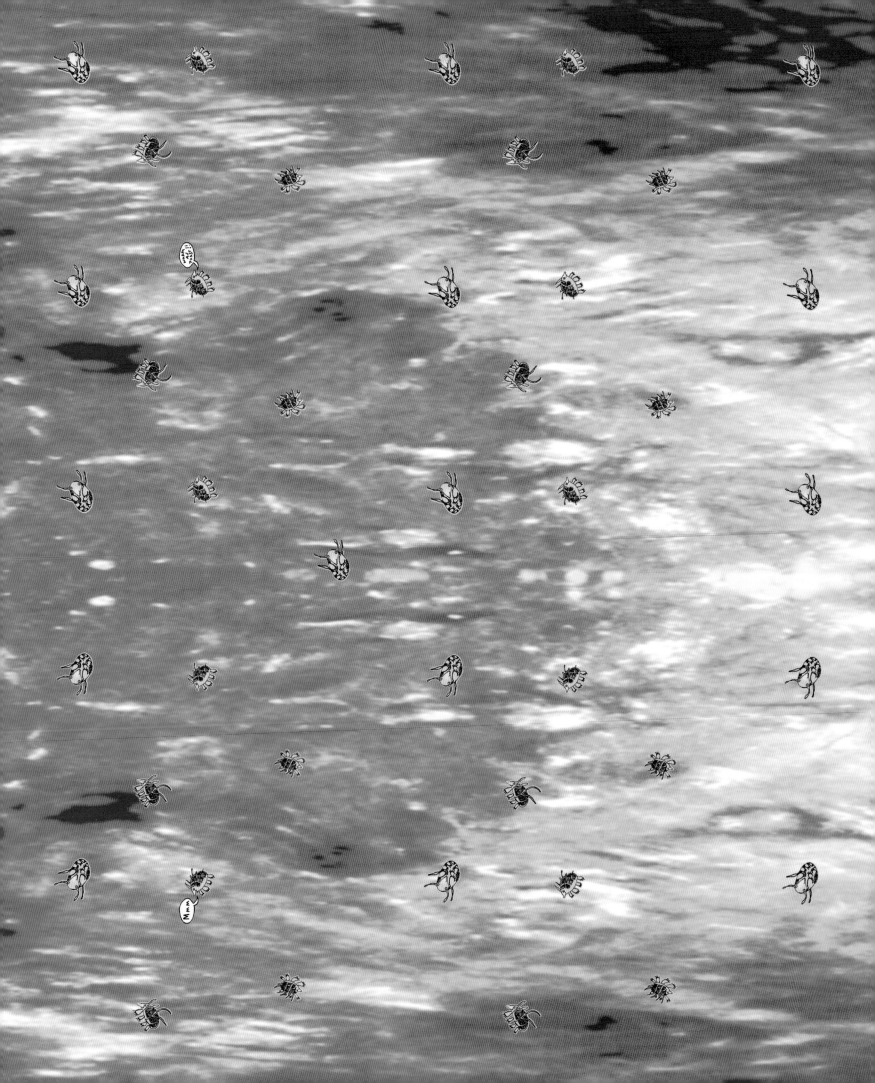

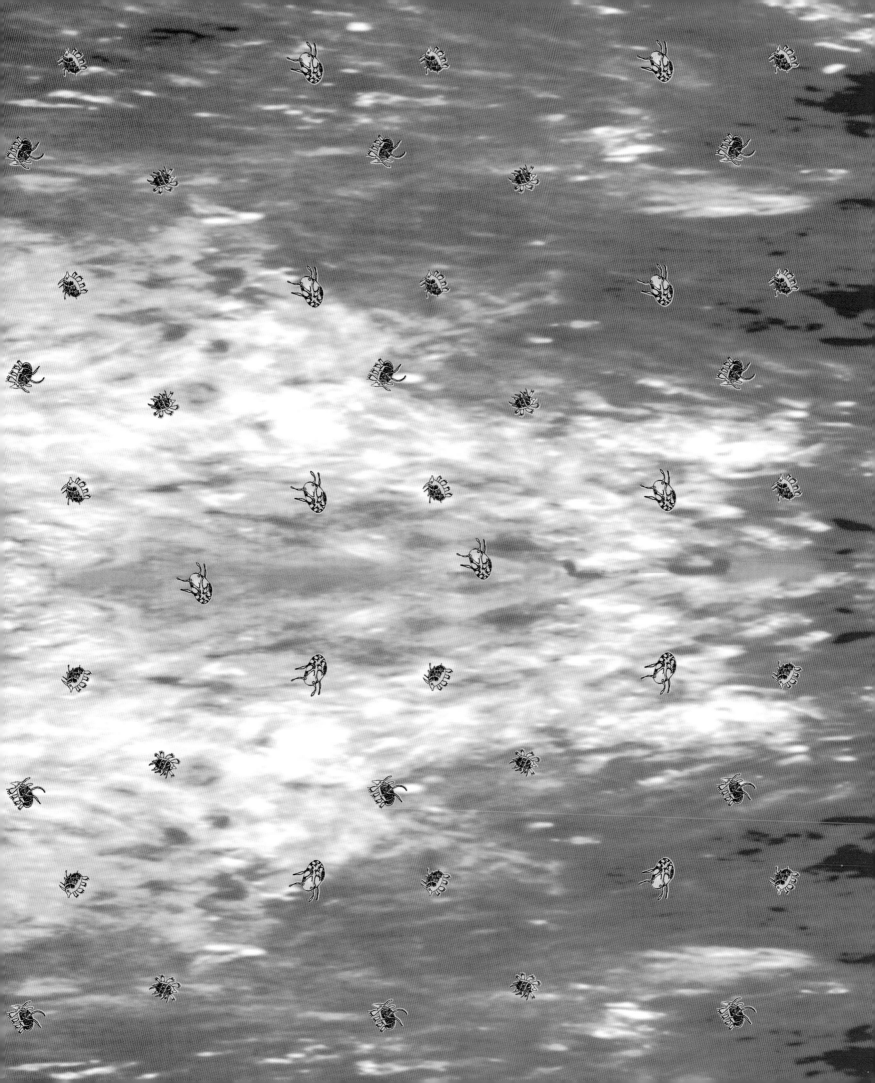

ANIMAL Science

HOW AND WHY ANIMALS DO THE THINGS THEY DO.

ANIMAL Science

SURVIVORS
THE TOUGHEST CREATURES ON EARTH

I THINK I CAN SEE SOMETHING...

NICOLA DAVIES
ILLUSTRATED BY NEAL LAYTON

ISBN 978-1-4063-5665-6

ANIMAL Science

POO
A NATURAL HISTORY OF THE UNMENTIONABLE

NICOLA DAVIES
ILLUSTRATED BY NEAL LAYTON

ISBN 978-1-4063-5663-2

ANIMAL Science

DEADLY!
THE TRUTH ABOUT THE MOST DANGEROUS CREATURES ON EARTH
NICOLA DAVIES   ILLUSTRATED BY NEAL LAYTON

ISBN 978-1-4063-5742-4

ANIMAL Science

TALK, TALK, SQUAWK!
HOW AND WHY ANIMALS COMMUNICATE

NICOLA DAVIES   ILLUSTRATED BY NEAL LAYTON

ISBN 978-1-4063-5748-6

ANIMAL Science

JUST THE RIGHT SIZE
WHY BIG ANIMALS ARE BIG AND LITTLE ANIMALS ARE LITTLE

NICOLA DAVIES
ILLUSTRATED BY NEAL LAYTON

ISBN 978-1-4063-5747-9

ANIMAL Science

WHAT'S EATING YOU?
PARASITES – THE INSIDE STORY
NICOLA DAVIES   ILLUSTRATED BY NEAL LAYTON

ISBN 978-1-4063-5664-9

If you enjoyed this book, why not collect them all!

Available from all good booksellers

www.walker.co.uk